WALKING IN DIVINE FAVOR

Other Books by the Author

The Minister's Handbook: A Guide for Leadership

Conducting Church Audits: A Guide for Internal Auditors

Preaching that Empowers God's People: Expository Preaching in the 21st Century

A Pastor's Introduction to Church Administration: Administering the 21st Century Church Effectively

A Charge to Preach: Letters to a Young Preacher

Unapologetically Baptist: A Biblical Exposition for New and Longtime Baptists

WALKING IN DIVINE FAVOR

A 30-DAY DEVOTIONAL JOURNEY OF GRACE AND REFLECTION

by

JEREMY W. ODOM

iPREACH
PUBLICATIONS

Dedication

To the beloved members of Saint Rest Baptist Church, whose unwavering faith and support have been a constant source of inspiration and strength.

And to all those seeking encouragement and renewal in their faith journey, may this book be a beacon of hope and a guide to deeper spiritual understanding.

Contents

INTRODUCTION

Welcome to **"Walking in God's Favor: A 30-Day Devotional Journey of Grace and Reflection."** This devotional is designed to guide you through a transformative journey of faith, helping you explore and experience the profound favor of God in your daily life.

In the hustle and bustle of modern life, it's easy to become overwhelmed by challenges and distractions. Yet, amidst the chaos, God's favor remains a constant source of strength, guidance, and blessing. This book aims to help you recognize and embrace that divine favor, offering you practical steps and spiritual insights to enrich your walk with God.

How to Use This Book

Over the next 30 days, you will embark on a daily devotional journey, each day focusing on one of the 30 Building Blocks of Favor. These principles are designed to help you deepen your faith, cultivate spiritual growth, and live a life that reflects the grace and blessings of God.

Each day's entry includes:

- **Scripture**: A verse from the Bible to ground your reflection in God's Word.
- **Reflection**: A brief meditation on the day's principle, offering insights and encouragement.
- **Journaling Prompt**: A question or thought to help you personalize the principle and apply it to your life.
- **Prayer**: A guided prayer to help you seek God's guidance and support.
- **Action Step**: A practical task to implement the day's principle, helping you actively live out your faith.

To get the most out of this devotional, set aside a quiet time each day for reflection and journaling. Allow yourself to engage deeply with the Scripture, the reflections, and the action steps. It is through this daily practice that you will begin to see and experience God's favor in new and profound ways.

A Journey of Grace

This journey is not just about personal growth but also about recognizing and responding to God's unending grace. As you navigate through these daily devotionals, you will uncover how God's favor shapes your life, guiding you towards His purpose and blessing.

Whether you are new to this spiritual practice or have been walking with God for years, this book is meant to be a companion on your journey. May it inspire you, challenge you, and bring you closer to the heart of God.

Thank you for choosing to embark on this journey of grace and reflection. May you experience the richness of God's favor and find renewed strength and hope as you walk with Him each day.

Blessings,

Jeremy W. Odom

DAY 1: REMEMBER THAT PRAYER IS THE ANSWER

"The prayer of a righteous person is powerful and effective."
- James 5:16

The Christian's most powerful resource is communion with God through prayer. It is through prayer that we tap into God's limitless power and wisdom. Many people mistakenly view prayer as a last resort, to be tried only when all other options have failed. This approach is backwards. Prayer should be our first response, not our last.

God's power is infinitely greater than our own, and He encourages us to rely on it. When we begin with prayer, we invite divine intervention and guidance into our situations, often leading to results far beyond our expectations. By prioritizing prayer, we align our hearts with God's will and open ourselves to His transformative influence in every aspect of our lives.

Action Step

Set aside a specific time each day for focused prayer. Begin today by writing out a prayer list of things you need guidance on or are thankful for and commit to praying over this list daily.

Prayer

Heavenly Father, thank You for the gift of prayer and the privilege of coming before You with our needs and concerns. Help me to remember that prayer is the answer to every challenge I face. Strengthen my faith and guide me as I seek Your will through prayer. May my conversations with You be filled with sincerity and trust, knowing that You are always listening and working for my good. Amen.

"Prayer does not change God, but it changes him who prays."
- Soren Kierkegaard

Your Journal Entry:

Reflect on a recent situation where prayer played a crucial role. How did it impact your situation? Write about a current challenge you are facing and how you plan to seek God's guidance through prayer.

DAY 2: STAND ON THE PROMISES OF GOD

"Through these he has given us his very great and precious promises, so that through them you may participate in the divine nature, having escaped the corruption in the world caused by evil desires."
- 2 Peter 1:4

The power to grow and live according to God's will doesn't come from within us, but from God Himself. We lack the inherent resources to embody "glory and virtue" on our own. Instead, God, in His grace, makes us "partakers of the divine nature" through His promises. This divine participation is essential for overcoming sin and living a life fully dedicated to Him.

When we are born again, God, through His Spirit, empowers us with His own moral goodness. His promises assure us of this divine assistance, which enables us to reflect His character and live in alignment with His will. Standing on His promises means relying on this supernatural strength and moral integrity that He provides, rather than our own limited resources.

Action Step

Identify a specific promise from God that resonates with you today. Write it down and meditate on it throughout the day. Reflect on how this promise can provide strength and guidance in your current situation.

Prayer

Lord, thank You for Your promises that provide us with hope and assurance. Help me to stand firm on Your promises, trusting in Your faithfulness even when circumstances seem difficult. Remind me of Your great and precious promises and let them be a source of strength and guidance in my life. Amen.

> *"God never made a promise that was too good to be true."*
> - Dwight L. Moody

Your Journal Entry:

Reflect on a time when standing on a promise from God made a difference in your life. How did it impact your situation? Write about a promise you are holding onto today and how it encourages you.

DAY 3: RECOGNIZE THE POWER INVESTED IN YOU

"Now to him who is able to do immeasurably more than all we ask or imagine, according to his power that is at work within us."
- Ephesians 3:20

Understanding and embracing the power that God has invested in you is crucial for living a victorious Christian life. Ephesians 3:20 reminds us that God is capable of exceeding our expectations and doing more than we can ask or imagine. This power is not distant or abstract; it is actively at work within us.

This divine power empowers you to overcome challenges, resist temptation, and fulfill your purpose. It is a power that transforms and equips you to live according to God's will. Recognizing this power involves acknowledging that you are not relying solely on your own strength but on the boundless power of God within you. Embracing this reality changes how you approach difficulties, pursue goals, and live out your faith.

Action Step

Reflect on areas of your life where you feel inadequate or overwhelmed. Consider how recognizing and relying on the power God has invested in you can change your approach to these challenges. Make a conscious effort to draw on this divine strength and power in your daily life and decision-making.

Prayer

Lord, thank You for the immeasurable power You have placed within me. Help me to recognize and embrace this divine strength in all areas of my life. Empower me to overcome challenges, resist temptation, and pursue Your will with confidence. Remind me daily that I am not alone but equipped with Your power to achieve more than I can imagine. Amen.

"God has not changed his mind: Despite delays, opposition, and bad breaks, God's plan is still going to happen."
- Unknown

Your Journal Entry:

Reflect on a current challenge or area in your life where you feel inadequate. How can recognizing the power God has invested in you help you approach this situation differently? Write about how you will rely on this divine strength in your daily life and decision-making. Consider specific ways to invite God's power into your circumstances.

DAY 4: ACKNOWLEDGE THE PRESENCE OF THE ADVERSARY

"Be alert and of sober mind. Your enemy the devil prowls around like a roaring lion looking for someone to devour."
- 1 Peter 5:8

Lions typically target the sick, young, or straggling animals—those that are alone or not alert. Similarly, Peter warns us that Satan prowls around, seeking those who are isolated or weakened by suffering and persecution. During such times, we may feel alone, weak, and cut off from the support of fellow believers. This vulnerability makes us especially susceptible to the adversary's attacks.

When we are focused solely on our troubles, we might forget to remain vigilant against danger. Peter's warning calls us to be alert, particularly when we are in distress. In these moments, it is crucial to seek support from other Christians, keep our eyes fixed on Christ, and actively resist the devil's schemes. By doing so, we can safeguard our faith and find strength in God's provision.

Action Step

Spend time in prayer asking God for strength and discernment to recognize when you are most vulnerable to the adversary's attacks. Reach out to fellow believers for support and encouragement. Write about any feelings of isolation or weakness you're experiencing and how you plan to stay vigilant and connected during these times.

Prayer

Heavenly Father, thank You for the warning about the adversary and for providing a way to protect ourselves through vigilance and community. Help me to stay alert, especially when I am feeling weak or isolated. Grant me the strength to resist Satan's attacks and the wisdom to seek support from other believers. Keep my eyes focused on You and guide me through my trials with Your grace and protection. Amen.

"The first step on the way to victory is to recognize the enemy."
- Martin Luther King, Jr.

Your Journal Entry:

Reflect on a time when you felt particularly vulnerable or isolated. How did this affect your faith and response to challenges? Write about ways you can seek support from other Christians and strategies to remain vigilant and focused on Christ during difficult times.

DAY 5: MAINTAIN YOUR DIGNITY

"She is clothed with strength and dignity; she can laugh at the days to come."
- Proverbs 31:25

Maintaining your dignity means upholding your moral and ethical standards, regardless of external circumstances. Dignity is about embodying inner strength and grace, not merely about appearance. While Proverbs 31 specifically describes a woman, the principles of strength and dignity are applicable to everyone.

Maintaining dignity involves living with integrity, even in challenging situations. It means responding to adversity with a calm spirit, making choices that reflect your values, and treating others with respect. By doing so, you reflect God's character and remain a positive witness of His grace and truth. Your dignity becomes a testament to your faith and trust in God's guidance.

Action Step

Reflect on an area in your life where you need to uphold your dignity. Identify specific actions or attitudes that might be compromising your integrity. Make a plan to address these issues and commit to living out your values with strength and grace.

Prayer

Lord, thank You for the example of dignity and strength in Your Word. Help me to maintain my dignity in all circumstances, responding with grace and integrity. Guide me in making choices that reflect Your character and uphold my values. Strengthen me to face challenges with confidence, knowing that my dignity is rooted in You. Amen.

"Without dignity, identity is erased. In its absence, men are defined not by themselves, but by their captors and the circumstances in which they are forced to live."
- Laura Hillenbrand

Your Journal Entry:

Reflect on a recent situation where maintaining your dignity was challenging. How did you respond, and what did you learn from the experience? Write about a specific area where you can improve in upholding your dignity and how you plan to act with integrity and grace moving forward.

DAY 6: UPGRADE YOUR ATMOSPHERE

"Finally, brothers and sisters, whatever is true, whatever is noble, whatever is right, whatever is pure, whatever is lovely, whatever is admirable—if anything is excellent or praiseworthy—think about such things."
- Philippians 4:8

What we put into our minds significantly influences our words and actions. Paul encourages us to fill our thoughts with what is true, noble, right, pure, lovely, and admirable. This practice involves not just considering what we think about but also evaluating what we consume through various media—television, music, books, movies, and magazines.

If you find yourself struggling with impure thoughts or daydreams, take a close look at what you are feeding your mind. Replace harmful or negative input with material that aligns with Philippians 4:8. This might mean choosing uplifting books, wholesome entertainment, and positive influences that reinforce your faith.

Above all, immerse yourself in God's Word and dedicate time to prayer. Ask God to help you focus on what is good and pure. Transforming your mental atmosphere is a process that requires effort and practice, but with God's help, it is achievable.

Action Step

Assess your current media and environmental inputs. Identify any sources that contribute negatively to your thoughts or spiritual well-being. Make a plan to replace these with positive, wholesome material. Commit to spending regular time in Scripture and prayer, asking God for guidance in focusing your mind on what is good and pure.

Prayer

Lord, help me to upgrade my atmosphere by filling my mind with thoughts that are true, noble, right, pure, lovely, and admirable. Guide me in choosing media and influences that support my spiritual growth. Strengthen me to replace harmful input with wholesome material and help me to focus on Your Word and in prayer. Transform my mind and actions to reflect Your goodness and purity. Amen.

"Acquire a taste for good thinking."
- Pastor Jonathan Hill

Your Journal Entry:

Reflect on the media and influences in your life. How do they affect your thoughts and actions? Write about the changes you plan to make in your environment and input to better align with Philippians 4:8. Describe how you will incorporate more positive, wholesome material and dedicate time to reading God's Word and praying.

DAY 7: PURGE YOUR LIFE OF USELESS SPACE

"Therefore, since we are surrounded by such a great cloud of witnesses, let us throw off everything that hinders and the sin that so easily entangles, and let us run with perseverance the race marked out for us."
- Hebrews 12:1

The Christian life involves hard work and intentional effort. It requires us to let go of anything that threatens our relationship with God. This includes not only sin but also distractions and burdens that impede our spiritual progress. To live effectively, we must run the race with patience, relying on the power of the Holy Spirit.

Keeping our eyes on Jesus is crucial; He is our ultimate focus and goal. When we shift our gaze away from Him—whether towards ourselves or our challenging circumstances—we risk stumbling and losing our way. The race we are running is for Christ, not for personal gain or self-satisfaction. By purging our lives of what hinders us and maintaining our focus on Jesus, we align ourselves with His purposes and run the race with perseverance and faithfulness.

Action Step

Identify one area in your life that may be distracting or hindering your spiritual journey. This could be a habit, a relationship, or a physical space that needs attention. Take specific steps to address and remove these obstacles, ensuring that your focus remains firmly on Christ.

Prayer

Lord, help me to recognize and eliminate anything in my life that endangers my relationship with You. Strengthen me to remove distractions and burdens that hinder my spiritual growth. Guide me to keep my eyes on Jesus, so that I may run the race You have set before me with perseverance and faithfulness. Amen.

"Nothing is impossible. The word itself says 'I'm possible!'"
- Audrey Hepburn

Your Journal Entry:

Reflect on a recent situation where you felt distracted or hindered in your spiritual journey. How did this affect your focus on Christ? Write about the steps you plan to take to remove these distractions and maintain a clear focus on Jesus in your daily life.

DAY 8: PRAISE GOD DAILY

"I will extol the Lord at all times; his praise will always be on my lips."
- Psalm 34:1

Praising God daily is a vital practice in cultivating a heart of gratitude and faith. Psalm 34:1 highlights the importance of constantly lifting our voices in praise, regardless of our circumstances. Praise is not just a response to blessings but a deliberate choice to acknowledge and honor God in every moment.

When we make praise a daily habit, we align our hearts with God's goodness and sovereignty. It shifts our focus from our problems to His faithfulness, reminding us of His unchanging nature and love. Praise also strengthens our relationship with God, fosters a positive outlook, and encourages us to trust Him more deeply.

Incorporating daily praise into your routine means finding moments throughout your day to worship God through prayer, song, or reflection. It transforms ordinary moments into opportunities for connecting with the divine and experiencing His presence more fully.

Action Step

Commit to setting aside specific times each day for praising God. This could be through prayer, singing, or reading Psalms. Reflect on how daily praise affects your perspective and relationship with God. Make a plan to incorporate this practice into your daily routine.

Prayer

Lord, I want to praise You at all times, as Your goodness and faithfulness deserve continual recognition. Help me to make praise a daily habit, regardless of my circumstances. Guide me in finding moments throughout my day to lift my voice and heart in worship to You. Transform my perspective through daily praise and deepen my relationship with You. Amen.

"Everything we do should glorify God."
- Billy Graham

Your Journal Entry:

Reflect on your current practice of praise. How often do you consciously praise God in your daily life? Write about the specific ways you will incorporate daily praise into your routine and the impact you expect it to have on your faith and outlook. Consider how this practice can transform your relationship with God and enhance your spiritual growth.

DAY 9: BE CALM AND LIVE

"Do not be anxious about anything, but in every situation, by prayer and petition, with thanksgiving, present your requests to God."
- Philippians 4:6

The Christian's most powerful resource is communion with God through prayer. Finding peace and calm in His presence involves turning to Him with our anxieties and concerns. Philippians 4:6 reminds us that instead of letting worry overwhelm us, we should present our requests to God with a thankful heart.

Many view prayer as a last resort, but it should be our first response. God's power far exceeds our own, and He invites us to rely on it. By prioritizing prayer, we invite His peace, which surpasses all understanding, into our lives. This approach helps us stay calm and centered, even when faced with stress and challenges.

Action Step

Practice a calming activity today, such as meditation, deep breathing, or quiet time with God. Use this time to focus on His promises and seek His peace amidst your daily challenges.

Prayer

Lord, I seek Your peace amidst my anxieties. Help me to turn to You first in prayer and thanksgiving, and to find calm in Your presence. Grant me Your peace that surpasses all understanding and guide me to trust in Your control over every situation in my life. Amen.

"Do not anticipate trouble or worry about what may never happen. Keep in the sunlight."
- Benjamin Franklin

Your Journal Entry:

Reflect on sources of stress in your life. How can you find calm in the midst of these challenges by turning to God in prayer and thanksgiving?

DAY 10: SHOW COMPASSION

"When he saw the crowds, he had compassion on them, because they were harassed and helpless, like sheep without a shepherd."
- Matthew 9:36

Compassion is a vital expression of God's love and mercy. In Matthew 9:36, Jesus observed the crowds and was deeply moved by their suffering and vulnerability. His compassion led Him to take action, healing and teaching those in need.

As followers of Christ, we are called to exhibit similar compassion in our interactions with others. Recognizing and responding to the struggles of those around us with empathy and kindness reflects God's love and concern. By showing compassion, we not only help alleviate others' burdens but also strengthen our own faith and relationships within our communities.

Action Step

Perform an act of compassion today. Whether it's offering a kind word, lending a helping hand, or showing understanding, let your actions mirror God's love and mercy towards others.

Prayer

Lord, give me a heart full of compassion, reflecting Your love and mercy. Help me to see the needs of those around me and respond with empathy and kindness. Guide me in performing acts of compassion that make a positive impact and show Your love to others. Amen.

*"There's something about compassion that causes society to say,
'We're going to take this person seriously.'"*
- Max Lucado

Journaling Prompt

Reflect on a recent act of compassion you witnessed or participated in. How did it impact you and the recipient? What did you learn from this experience about showing compassion?

DAY 11: DEVELOP GRATITUDE

"Give thanks in all circumstances; for this is God's will for you in Christ Jesus."
- 1 Thessalonians 5:18

Developing gratitude involves cultivating a mindset that recognizes and appreciates God's blessings in every situation. 1 Thessalonians 5:18 instructs us to give thanks in all circumstances, not just the favorable ones. This practice helps shift our focus from what we lack to the abundance we have received from God.

Gratitude transforms our perspective, enabling us to see God's hand in both the highs and lows of life. It reinforces our trust in His provision and care, fostering a deeper relationship with Him. By regularly expressing thanks, we align ourselves with God's will and build a positive, faith-filled attitude.

Action Step

Take time today to list specific things you are grateful for. Make a habit of expressing your thanks to God for these blessings, and let this practice enhance your awareness of His goodness in your life.

Prayer

Lord, help me to develop a heart of gratitude, recognizing Your blessings in all circumstances. Teach me to give thanks not only for the good times but also for the challenges, knowing that You work through both to shape my life. Fill me with Your peace and joy as I cultivate this grateful mindset. Amen.

"Gratitude is a currency that we can mint for ourselves, and spend without fear of bankruptcy."
- Fred De Witt Van Amburgh

Journaling Prompt

Reflect on recent situations where you found it challenging to be thankful. How can developing a habit of gratitude change your perspective and enhance your relationship with God?

DAY 12: PURSUE RIGHTEOUSNESS

"Flee the evil desires of youth and pursue righteousness, faith, love, and peace, along with those who call on the Lord out of a pure heart."
- 2 Timothy 2:22

Pursuing righteousness involves a deliberate effort to live in a way that reflects God's character and desires. 2 Timothy 2:22 urges us to flee from youthful temptations and instead chase after righteousness, faith, love, and peace. This pursuit is a proactive journey, not just about avoiding sin but actively seeking to embody Christ-like qualities.

Righteousness requires commitment and a heart aligned with God's will. Engaging in practices that foster spiritual growth, such as studying Scripture and maintaining fellowship with other believers, supports this pursuit. By focusing on these virtues, we align our lives more closely with God's standards and experience His transforming power.

Action Step

Identify areas in your life where you can more actively pursue righteousness. Set practical goals to improve in these areas, such as regular Bible study, prayer, and engaging with a supportive faith community.

Prayer

Lord, guide me in my pursuit of righteousness. Help me to turn away from desires that lead me astray and to earnestly seek faith, love, and peace. Surround me with others who share this pursuit and strengthen my resolve to live a life that reflects Your character. Amen.

"Better to spend a lifetime struggling toward perfection than to give up the pursuit altogether."
- Tripp Prince

Journaling Prompt

Reflect on specific areas where you need to pursue righteousness more diligently. What steps can you take to align your actions and thoughts with God's will?

DAY 13: SEEK WISDOM CONTINUALLY

"If any of you lacks wisdom, you should ask God, who gives generously to all without finding fault, and it will be given to you."
- James 1:5

Seeking wisdom continually means recognizing our need for divine guidance in every aspect of life. James 1:5 assures us that God generously provides wisdom to those who ask. Wisdom is essential for making decisions that align with God's will and navigating life's challenges.

By consistently seeking God's wisdom through prayer, studying Scripture, and seeking counsel from mature believers, we open ourselves to His guidance and insight. This continual pursuit of wisdom equips us to live according to God's purposes and make choices that honor Him.

Action Step

Commit to a daily practice of seeking God's wisdom. Spend time in prayer and Scripture reading, asking for His guidance in the decisions you face.

Prayer

Lord, grant me Your wisdom as I navigate life's decisions and challenges. Help me to seek Your guidance continually and to trust in Your insight. Guide me in making choices that align with Your will and honor You. Amen.

"The first problem for all of us, men and women, is not to learn, but to unlearn."
- Gloria Steinem

Journaling Prompt

Reflect on a recent decision where you sought God's wisdom. How did His guidance impact your choice and its outcome?

DAY 14: PURSUE PEACE

"Let us therefore make every effort to do what leads to peace and to mutual edification."
- Romans 14:19

Pursuing peace involves actively working towards harmonious relationships and resolving conflicts. Romans 14:19 encourages us to strive for peace and build up one another. This pursuit requires intentional actions, such as seeking reconciliation and fostering understanding in our interactions.

By prioritizing peace, we contribute to a positive and supportive environment that reflects God's love and grace. This effort not only benefits our relationships but also aligns us with God's desire for unity and harmony within the body of Christ.

Action Step

Identify a current conflict or area of tension in your relationships. Take steps today to address it and work towards a peaceful resolution.

Prayer

Lord, help me to pursue peace in all my relationships and interactions. Guide me in resolving conflicts and fostering understanding, and let Your peace be evident in my actions and words. Amen.

"For it isn't enough to talk about peace. One must believe in it. And it isn't enough to believe in it. One must work at it."
- Eleanor Roosevelt

Journaling Prompt

Reflect on a recent situation where you actively pursued peace. What was the outcome, and how did it affect your relationships and personal growth?

DAY 15: SHOW HOSPITALITY

"Do not forget to show hospitality to strangers, for by so doing some people have shown hospitality to angels without knowing it."
- Hebrews 13:2

Showing hospitality is a tangible expression of God's love and kindness. Hebrews 13:2 highlights the importance of welcoming others, including strangers, and treating them with warmth and generosity. Hospitality opens doors for meaningful connections and demonstrates our care for others.

By being hospitable, we reflect God's welcoming nature and create opportunities to bless others. This act of kindness can have a profound impact, offering support and creating bonds that enrich our communities and our own spiritual journey.

Action Step

Extend hospitality to someone today, whether by inviting them into your home, sharing a meal, or offering a helping hand. Let this act of kindness reflect God's love.

Prayer

Lord, help me to show genuine hospitality to others. May my actions reflect Your love and warmth, and may I be a blessing to those I welcome into my life. Amen.

"People will forget what you said. They will forget what you did. But they will never forget how you made them feel."
- Maya Angelou

Journaling Prompt

Reflect on a time when someone showed hospitality to you. How did it impact you, and how can you apply that experience to your own practice of hospitality?

DAY 16: ENGAGE IN SERVICE

"You, my brothers and sisters, were called to be free. But do not use your freedom to indulge the flesh; rather, serve one another humbly in love."
- Galatians 5:13

Engaging in service reflects our commitment to live out God's love by putting others' needs before our own. Galatians 5:13 reminds us that our freedom in Christ is intended for serving others humbly and lovingly.

Service can take many forms, from volunteering in our communities to supporting those in need. By engaging in service, we demonstrate our faith through actions and contribute to building a more compassionate and supportive world.

Action Step

Identify a way you can serve others today. Whether through volunteering, helping a neighbor, or supporting a community project, let your service reflect God's love.

Prayer

Lord, guide me in finding opportunities to serve others. Help me to approach service with humility and love, reflecting Your grace and making a positive impact in my community. Amen.

"Service to others is the rent you pay for your room here on Earth."
- Muhammad Ali

Journaling Prompt

Reflect on a recent experience where you engaged in service. How did it affect you and the people you served? What did you learn from this experience?

DAY 17: BE A PEACEMAKER

"Blessed are the peacemakers, for they will be called children of God."
- Matthew 5:9

Being a peacemaker involves actively working to resolve conflicts and foster reconciliation. Matthew 5:9 highlights the blessing and honor of those who strive to bring peace and harmony. Peacemaking requires empathy, patience, and a willingness to address and resolve disputes constructively.

As peacemakers, we reflect God's nature and contribute to a more harmonious environment. This role not only benefits those around us but also deepens our relationship with God as we live out His command to seek peace.

Action Step

Identify a conflict or tension in your life or community. Take steps to mediate and resolve the issue, focusing on fostering understanding and reconciliation.

Prayer

Lord, make me a peacemaker in my relationships and community. Help me to approach conflicts with grace and understanding, seeking to bring about reconciliation and harmony. Amen.

"Not one of us can rest, be happy, be at home, be at peace with ourselves, until we end hatred and division."
- John Lewis

Journaling Prompt

Reflect on a recent situation where you acted as a peacemaker. What challenges did you face, and how did it affect the outcome of the conflict?

DAY 18: GIVE LIBERALLY

"Each of you should give what you have decided in your heart to give, not reluctantly or under compulsion, for God loves a cheerful giver."
- 2 Corinthians 9:7

Giving liberally involves sharing our resources with others generously and joyfully. 2 Corinthians 9:7 emphasizes that our giving should come from a willing heart, not out of obligation. When we give cheerfully, we reflect God's generosity and trust in His provision.

Generous giving extends beyond financial contributions to include time, talents, and support for those in need. By giving liberally, we contribute to God's work and bless others, fostering a spirit of abundance and gratitude.

Action Step

Find a way to give generously today, whether through a financial donation, volunteering time, or offering support to someone in need. Let your giving reflect a joyful and willing heart.

Prayer

Lord, guide me in giving generously and cheerfully. Help me to share my resources with a willing heart and to trust in Your provision. May my giving reflect Your love and grace. Amen.

"We make a living by what we get, but we make a life by what we give."
- Winston Churchill

Journaling Prompt

Reflect on a recent act of giving. How did it affect you and the recipient? What did you learn about the impact of generous giving?

DAY 19: FOSTER COMMUNITY

"All the believers were together and had everything in common. They sold property and possessions to give to anyone who had need. Every day they continued to meet together in the temple courts; they broke bread in their homes and ate together with glad and sincere hearts, praising God and enjoying the favor of all the people."
- Acts 2:44-47

Fostering community involves building strong, supportive relationships within the body of Christ. Acts 2:44-47 describes the early church's commitment to living in unity, sharing resources, and supporting each other. This example shows the importance of communal living and mutual care in the Christian faith.

By actively participating in and nurturing our community, we create a space where believers can grow, support one another, and share in God's blessings. This communal spirit strengthens our faith and deepens our connections with others.

Action Step

Engage with your faith community today by participating in a group activity, offering support to a fellow believer, or organizing a gathering to foster connections.

Prayer

Lord, help me to actively contribute to building and nurturing my faith community. Guide me in offering support, sharing resources, and fostering strong, meaningful relationships with others. Amen.

"Strong communities are born out of individuals being their best selves."
- Leanne Betasamosake Simpson

Journaling Prompt

Reflect on your involvement in your faith community. How can you contribute more effectively to building a supportive and connected environment?

DAY 20: DEMONSTRATE FAITHFULNESS

"Now it is required that those who have been given a trust must prove faithful."
- 1 Corinthians 4:2

Demonstrating faithfulness involves consistently fulfilling our responsibilities and commitments in accordance with God's expectations. 1 Corinthians 4:2 highlights the importance of being trustworthy and reliable in the roles and responsibilities entrusted to us.

Faithfulness is reflected in our daily actions, choices, and interactions. By being steadfast and dependable, we honor God and build trust with others, reflecting His faithfulness in our lives.

Action Step

Identify an area where you need to demonstrate greater faithfulness. Take concrete steps to fulfill your responsibilities and commitments with diligence and integrity.

Prayer

Lord, help me to be faithful in all areas of my life. Strengthen my resolve to meet my responsibilities with integrity and dedication, reflecting Your faithfulness in my actions. Amen.

"Be faithful in small things because it is in them that your strength lies."
- Mother Teresa

Journaling Prompt

Reflect on a recent situation where you demonstrated faithfulness. How did it impact you and those around you? What did you learn from this experience?

DAY 21: SEEK TO UNDERSTAND

"The beginning of wisdom is this: Get wisdom. Though it cost all you have, get understanding."
- Proverbs 4:7

Seeking to understand involves striving to gain insight and empathy in our interactions with others. Proverbs 4:7 underscores the value of understanding as a cornerstone of wisdom. This pursuit requires active listening, openness, and a willingness to consider different perspectives.

By seeking to understand others, we build stronger relationships and foster a more compassionate and informed approach to our interactions. This effort enhances our ability to relate to and support those around us.

Action Step

Make an effort today to understand someone else's perspective or situation. Practice active listening and ask questions to gain deeper insight into their thoughts and feelings.

Prayer

Lord, grant me the wisdom and patience to seek to understand others more deeply. Help me to listen actively and empathetically, and to build connections based on mutual understanding and respect. Amen.

"The great art of learning is to understand but little at a time."
- John Locke

Journaling Prompt

Reflect on a recent interaction where you sought to understand someone else's perspective. How did this approach affect the outcome of the conversation and your relationship?

DAY 22: EMBRACE NEW BEGINNINGS

"See, I am doing a new thing! Now it springs up; do you not perceive it? I am making a way in the wilderness and streams in the wasteland."
- Isaiah 43:19

Embracing new beginnings involves being open to the transformative work that God is doing in our lives. Isaiah 43:19 speaks of God's ability to create new paths and opportunities even in challenging situations. Embracing these new beginnings requires faith and a willingness to step into the unknown with trust in God's plan.

By accepting and welcoming the new things God is doing, we align ourselves with His work and open ourselves to growth and renewal. This mindset allows us to move forward with hope and expectation.

Action Step

Identify a new beginning in your life that you may be hesitant to embrace. Take a step forward with faith, trusting that God is guiding you and making a way.

Prayer

Lord, help me to embrace the new beginnings You are bringing into my life. Give me the courage and faith to step forward with trust in Your plan and to welcome the changes You are orchestrating. Amen.

"Your future is created by what you do today, not tomorrow."

- Robert Kiyosaki

Journaling Prompt

Reflect on a recent new beginning you embraced. How did this experience affect your faith and outlook on life?

DAY 23: EMBRACE SIMPLICITY

"But godliness with contentment is great gain. For we brought nothing into the world, and we can take nothing out of it. But if we have food and clothing, we will be content with that."
- 1 Timothy 6:6-8

Embracing simplicity involves finding contentment in what we have and focusing on what truly matters. 1 Timothy 6:6-8 emphasizes the value of godliness coupled with contentment, recognizing that our worth and fulfillment do not come from material possessions but from our relationship with God. Simplicity helps us prioritize our spiritual well-being over the pursuit of wealth and status.

By simplifying our lives, we make space for deeper connections with God and others, and we cultivate a sense of peace and satisfaction.

Action Step

Identify areas in your life where you might be overcomplicating things or pursuing material gain. Take steps to simplify and focus on what truly brings you contentment and spiritual growth.

Prayer

Lord, help me to embrace simplicity and find contentment in Your provision. Guide me in simplifying my life to focus on what truly matters and to cultivate a deeper relationship with You. Amen.

"I make myself rich, by making my wants few."
- Henry David Thoreau

Journaling Prompt

Reflect on a recent decision where you embraced simplicity. How did this choice impact your sense of contentment and your relationship with God?

DAY 24: EMBRACE CONTENTMENT

"I am not saying this because I am in need, for I have learned to be content whatever the circumstances. I know what it is to be in need, and I know what it is to have plenty. I have learned the secret of being content in any and every situation, whether well fed or hungry, whether living in plenty or in want. I can do all this through him who gives me strength."
- Philippians 4:11-13

Contentment involves finding satisfaction and peace regardless of your circumstances. Philippians 4:11-13 teaches us that true contentment comes from relying on Christ's strength rather than our own circumstances. By embracing contentment, we focus on what we have rather than what we lack, and we trust in God's provision.

This perspective shifts our focus from external conditions to internal peace and reliance on Christ, fostering a more stable and grateful heart.

Action Step

Identify areas where you struggle with discontentment. Practice gratitude and rely on Christ's strength to find satisfaction in your current circumstances.

Prayer

Lord, help me to embrace contentment in all circumstances. Teach me to find satisfaction in Your provision and to rely on Your strength rather than my own. Amen.

"Great leaders understand that historical success tends to produce stable and inwardly focused organizations, and these outfits, in turn, reinforce a feeling of contentment with the status quo."
- John P. Kotter

Journaling Prompt

Reflect on a recent experience where you learned to be content. How did this shift in perspective affect your attitude and relationship with God?

DAY 25: CULTIVATE PATIENCE

"You too, be patient and stand firm, because the Lord's coming is near."
- James 5:8

Cultivating patience involves enduring challenges and waiting on God's timing with trust and perseverance. James 5:8 encourages us to be patient and steadfast, especially in times of difficulty or waiting. Patience allows us to grow spiritually and remain steadfast in our faith.

By cultivating patience, we demonstrate trust in God's plan and timing, and we develop a deeper reliance on His guidance and provision.

Action Step

Identify an area in your life where you are struggling with impatience. Practice patience by taking specific steps to wait on God's timing and to trust in His plan.

Prayer

Lord, help me to cultivate patience in my life and to stand firm in my faith. Teach me to trust in Your timing and to remain steadfast through challenges. Amen.

"To lose patience is to lose the battle."
- Mahatma Gandhi

Journaling Prompt

Reflect on a recent situation where you practiced patience. How did this experience impact your faith and your ability to wait on God's timing?

DAY 26: HOLD ONTO YOUR HOPE

"May the God of hope fill you with all joy and peace as you trust in him, so that you may overflow with hope by the power of the Holy Spirit."
- Romans 15:13

Holding onto hope involves maintaining a confident expectation in God's promises and His ability to fulfill them. Romans 15:13 highlights that God, as the source of hope, fills us with joy and peace when we trust in Him. This hope is not merely wishful thinking, but a powerful assurance grounded in God's faithfulness.

By holding onto this hope, we experience spiritual renewal and strength, even in difficult times. It enables us to face challenges with a positive and trusting outlook.

Action Step

Reflect on an area of your life where you need to hold onto hope. Pray for God's strength and assurance and take steps to reinforce your hope through His promises and faithfulness.

Prayer

Lord, fill me with Your hope and strengthen my faith in Your promises. Help me to hold onto this hope in all circumstances and to find joy and peace through my trust in You. Amen.

"We must accept finite disappointment, but never lose infinite hope."
- Martin Luther King, Jr.

Journaling Prompt

Reflect on a time when holding onto hope made a difference in your life. How did it impact your perspective and your actions?

DAY 27: EMBRACE FORGIVENESS

"Bear with each other and forgive one another if any of you has a grievance against someone. Forgive as the Lord forgave you."
- Colossians 3:13

Embracing forgiveness involves letting go of grudges and extending grace to others as God has done for us. Colossians 3:13 calls us to forgive others just as we have been forgiven by the Lord. This act of forgiveness is essential for maintaining healthy relationships and reflecting God's love.

Forgiveness frees us from the burden of anger and resentment, allowing us to experience peace and reconciliation. It also aligns us with God's example of grace and mercy.

Action Step

Identify someone you need to forgive and take steps to extend grace to them. Pray for the strength and willingness to let go of any lingering grievances.

Prayer

Lord, help me to embrace forgiveness and extend grace to those who have wronged me. Heal my heart from any bitterness and guide me in reflecting Your forgiveness in my relationships. Amen.

"Forgiveness is about empowering yourself, rather than empowering your past."
- T. D. Jakes

Journaling Prompt

Reflect on a recent experience where you extended forgiveness. How did it affect your relationship with the person and your own sense of peace?

DAY 28: SEEK GOD'S GUIDANCE

"Trust in the Lord with all your heart and lean not on your own understanding; in all your ways submit to him, and he will make your paths straight."
- Proverbs 3:5-6

Seeking God's guidance involves trusting Him completely and submitting to His will in all aspects of our lives. Proverbs 3:5-6 emphasizes the importance of relying on God rather than our own understanding. By submitting our plans and decisions to God, we invite His wisdom and direction into our lives.

Seeking His guidance helps us make choices that align with His will and leads us on a path of righteousness and fulfillment.

Action Step

Pray for God's guidance in a specific area of your life. Seek His wisdom through Scripture, prayer, and counsel from others who are spiritually mature.

Prayer

Lord, I trust in Your wisdom and guidance for my life. Help me to seek You in all my decisions and to rely on Your understanding rather than my own. Direct my paths and lead me according to Your will. Amen.

"I do not pretend to be a divine man, but I do believe in divine guidance, divine power, and in the fulfilment of divine prophecy."
- Malcolm X

Journaling Prompt

Reflect on a recent decision where you sought God's guidance. How did this process affect the outcome and your sense of direction?

DAY 29: REFLECT ON YOUR JOURNEY

"I will remember the deeds of the Lord; yes, I will remember your miracles of long ago. I will consider all your works and meditate on all your mighty deeds."
- Psalm 77:11-12

Taking time to reflect on your journey is an important practice in the Christian faith. Psalm 77:11-12 encourages us to remember and meditate on the deeds and miracles of the Lord. Reflecting on where you've been, what you've experienced, and how God has worked in your life provides a deeper understanding of His faithfulness and guidance.

As you review your journey, consider the lessons learned, the challenges overcome, and the growth achieved. This reflection not only helps you appreciate God's work in your life but also prepares you for future steps in your faith journey.

Action Step

Set aside time today to review the past 29 days. Reflect on your experiences, insights, and growth. Write down the key moments where you saw God's hand at work and consider how these experiences have shaped your faith. Share these reflections with a trusted friend or mentor.

Prayer

Lord, thank You for the journey I've been on over the past 29 days. Help me to see and appreciate Your work in my life. Guide me as I reflect on my experiences and grow in my understanding of Your faithfulness. Amen.

"In the end, it's not the years in your life that count. It's the life in your years."
- Abraham Lincoln

Journaling Prompt

Reflect on your spiritual journey over the past month. What significant moments stand out to you? How have these moments impacted your faith and perspective? Write about how you've seen God's hand at work in your life.

DAY 30: CELEBRATE YOUR PROGRESS

"The Lord has done great things for us, and we are filled with joy."
- Psalm 126:3

Celebrating progress is an essential part of the Christian journey. Psalm 126:3 reminds us that recognizing and rejoicing in the great things God has done in our lives brings joy and gratitude. Reflecting on how far you've come, the growth you've experienced, and the ways God has worked in your life helps to reinforce your faith and encourages you to continue in your spiritual walk.

It's important to take time to acknowledge your progress and celebrate the milestones, both big and small. This practice not only fosters a sense of accomplishment but also deepens your appreciation for God's faithfulness and provision.

Action Step

Take some time today to review your journey over the past 30 days. Reflect on the changes you've made, the lessons you've learned, and the growth you've experienced. Celebrate these achievements with gratitude and joy and consider sharing your reflections with someone who can rejoice with you.

Prayer

Lord, thank You for the progress and growth You've allowed me to experience over these 30 days. Help me to celebrate Your goodness and faithfulness in my life. Guide me as I continue to grow and seek Your will. Amen.

"Without continual growth and progress, such words as improvement, achievement and success have no meaning."
- Benjamin Franklin

Journaling Prompt

Reflect on your journey over the past 30 days. What progress have you made? How has your faith grown? Write about the milestones you've reached and the ways you've seen God's hand at work in your life.

Journaling Tips

Journaling is a powerful tool for spiritual growth and reflection. Here are some tips to help you make the most of your journaling experience:

1. Set a Regular Time

Consistency helps in making journaling a habit. Find a time each day that works best for you—whether it's in the morning, during lunch, or before bed—and stick to it. This routine helps create a dedicated space for reflection and prayer.

2. Create a Quiet Space

Choose a comfortable, quiet spot where you can focus without distractions. This could be a special corner in your home, a peaceful outdoor setting, or anywhere you feel relaxed and can concentrate on your thoughts and prayers.

3. Be Honest and Open

Write freely and honestly about your thoughts, feelings, and experiences. This journal is a personal space for you to communicate with God and reflect on your spiritual journey. Don't worry about grammar or structure—focus on expressing your heart.

4. Use Prompts for Guidance

If you find yourself stuck or unsure where to start, use the journaling prompts provided in each daily entry. These prompts are designed to guide your reflection and help you explore different aspects of your spiritual journey.

5. Reflect on Scripture

Consider the Bible verses provided for each day as you journal. Reflect on how these scriptures relate to your experiences and thoughts. Write down any insights or revelations you gain from your study of God's Word.

6. Record Your Prayers

Use your journal to record your prayers, including your requests, thanks, and any specific praises. Keeping track of your prayers helps you see how God answers them over time and builds your faith in His provision and guidance.

7. Celebrate Your Progress

Take note of your spiritual milestones and growth. Acknowledge and celebrate the progress you've made, no matter how small. This practice helps reinforce positive changes and encourages you to keep moving forward in your faith journey.

8. Review and Reflect

Periodically review your journal entries to see how you've grown and what you've learned. Reflecting on past entries can provide encouragement and insight into your spiritual development.

9. Keep It Private

Remember that your journal is a personal space for your thoughts and reflections. Keep it private to ensure that you feel free to express yourself honestly and openly without concern.

10. Be Patient with Yourself

Journaling is a process that evolves over time. Be patient with yourself as you develop this practice. It's okay if some days are more challenging than others. Trust that God is working in and through your journaling efforts.